Yearly Reflections at Christmas

Debra Downey-Stockdale

WestBow Press books may be ordered through booksellers or by contacting:

WestBow Press
A Division of Thomas Nelson & Zondervan
1663 Liberty Drive
Bloomington, IN 47403
www.westbowpress.com
1 (866) 928-1240

ISBN: 978-1-9736-7086-5 (sc)
ISBN: 978-1-9736-7085-8 (e)

Print information available on the last page.

WestBow Press rev. date: 09/06/2019

Contents

Acknowledgements

With special thanks:

- I do give foremost, my praise and thanksgiving to the Lord Jesus Christ for this book – for I owe my very being and who I have become to Him.
- Secondly, my Mom, who always let me dream and express myself in various ways, and who was such a creative and fun person. Whom, I had the joy of leading her to receive the Christmas gift of Jesus shortly before her passing. See you soon Mom, I know you would be thrilled to have my book!
- Of course, I am also thankful to my wonderful daughter Kate and close friends Rita Trolley, Christine Dejager, Connie Goodson, Catherine Fraser, Beth Cockburn, Laurie Bigelow who prayed so much for me each year – believing and supporting me in this mission to share the gift of life that came at Christmas.
- I also want to thank Deborra Moore who gladly agreed to proof (patience of Job), Barb Link in helping me to tackle in a manageable way the overwhelming submission requirements, my daughter Kate Weiss who assisted and critiqued all the additional material requirements along with Laurie Bigelow jumpstarting the process with some creative input.

Preface

For as long as I can remember, I loved to express myself in writing as I was such a dreamer. There was such a strong sense that there was more to life than my own little world and at times it was my escape! However, the tug of God pulled at my heart at a young age and eventually I came to have a personal relationship with Him. It had its ups and downs as I grew up and eventually took hold of me in a deep relationship with Him through His Son Jesus Christ.

The Christmas Poetry came through a desire to share that wonderful Christmas gift God gave of His Son with others – as it alone brings lasting hope, life, and joy this world cannot impart. I can't say I kept all of them, I didn't start with a plan to write a book.... However, you will note as you read, there is a progressive change. Starting off with simple poems to ones of a deeper personal wrestling and acknowledgement of what effect this gift truly makes in a life. I have to admit it was a struggle every year to do this, much prayer, fasting, reading His word and WAITING on His message.

May God prepare your heart as you read His truth and message of hope He has for you.

For His Glory,

Debra Downey-Stockdale

Awake O Christian!

For God so loved the world that He sent His very best,
Which put the gates of darkness in turmoil and unrest,
For God's plan of salvation was soon to be fulfilled,
While Satan sought ways for Jesus to be killed.

Today the baby Jesus a story that is told,
Around the world to many, indifferent and cold,
Rejoicing in the season, yet no true joy within,
Lost, deceived and dying, eternally in their sin.

Christians, O Christ's ones so many times swept along,
The current of complacency where they don't belong,
While Christ watches and grieves for their love divided so,
Amidst themselves with all the worldly glitter and glow.

Awake, awake O Christian, this very day, today!
For Satan desires to have you travel on his way,
Ways of apathy, self-interest, idols or good works,
Building self-exaltation where his evil networks.

Victory can be yours if you yield control each day,
To God's spirit of truth to guide you along the way,
Take captive your thoughts to make them obey,
Then closer you will become to His image each day.

Hail to the Prince of Peace sent down from heaven above,
Who gives the power to live in all God's grace and love,
Defeated O Satan, Christ's ones we have naught to fear,
Christ our Saviour forever to all who draw near.

Living His Truth

Do you know and live for The Christ all year round?
Does His love and spirit in your life abound?
Do you practice living by His guiding hand?
Or do you coast along not taking a stand?

Is your life His light for people to see and follow?
Or does it shine forth only the flesh so vain, so hollow?
Oh confess all your sins, be quick to repent,
Put on your armour, the day is almost spent.

Bow down to His Lordship daily in your life,
Know the victory over all your sin and strife,
Christ's coming is nigh, our deliverance at hand,
Live for His glory and by His truth ye shall stand!

> "Then you will know the truth, and the truth will set you free."
> John 8:32

For Hope Does Not Disappoint

Thank you for the hope You sent 2000 years ago,
Hope that spanned the course of time from such a manger low,
Hope that sent your Son to die upon Golgotha's tree,
Who paid the debt and now lives to give the victory.

Hope beyond all sin and death to a life forever,
Captives freed from their chains that only God can sever,
O what blessed hope this is, a joy beyond compare,
That those who believe in Christ and live for Him can share.

Hope that calls discouraged hearts to press on and believe,
That here is just a breath away from heaven to receive,
Now to walk by faith not sight, God's Word our light and guide,
Jesus our hope - Awake! He comes quickly for His Bride!

> "For God so loved the world that He gave His one and only Son, that whoever believes in Him shall not perish but have eternal life." John 3:16
>
> "May the God of hope fill you with all joy and peace as you trust in Him, so that you may overflow with hope by the power of the Holy Spirit." Romans 15:13

O Morning Star I Await Thee

Rejoice, rejoice with hosts of angels on high,
The Saviour was born that we may live and not die,
All praise to the Father whose love draws mankind,
To a gift of salvation in Christ only, we'll find.

Praise to The Lord who grants mercy and grace,
Through His Only Son to a fallen race,
Born of a virgin sent from Heaven above,
So pure and so Holy and filled with God's love.

O sweet gentle Babe to grow to be a man,
To fulfill in life and death all of God's plan,
To rise again and to live forever free,
Where O death is thy sting, where thy victory?

Son of The Most High, yet so lowly and meek,
Offering hope to all the lost that would seek,
Forgiveness and healing found in Him alone,
For the debt of man's sin Jesus did atone.

All Hail King Jesus! soon to come once again,
Gathering all His own in a victor's train,
All tears, pain, death and sorrow will be gone,
PROCLAIM! The Morning Star appears come the Dawn!

Look Up! The Star is Still Shining!

Little star o'er Bethlehem, you shine to beckon all,
That Jesus Christ, God's own Son has come to yonder stall,
To change the course of all mankind never seen before,
Rejoice O ye fallen race, come yon to stable door.

There lies within Heaven's delight of God's plan fulfilled,
O bow down to your Saviour and let your tongues be stilled,
Peace has come for troubled hearts that long for perfect rest,
And those who search for life and truth can now end their quest.

O such love that came to dwell with sinners such as we,
Rejected, despised and nailed upon Calvary's tree,
To pay our debt, set us free and take our guilt and shame,
For the Christ Child brings deliverance, JESUS is His name!

> "For unto us a child is born, to us a Son is given, and the government will be upon His shoulders, and He will be called Wonderful Counsellor, Mighty God, Everlasting Father, Prince of Peace." Isaiah 9:6

To Him Who Overcomes

Return me to the manger where hope began so small,
To fall upon my knees dear Lord and harken to Your call,
Repenting of my wayward heart, to live for You today,
Knowing that Your death brought life and opened heaven's way.

The Alpha, The Omega, The Bright and Morning Star,
Bringing good tidings of hope from glories afar,
O praise to The Saviour who overcame sin and death,
Who forever reigns, offering salvation, life and breath.

O precious Lamb of God, You understand and know,
How weak Your children are and their need of You so,
Bent on destruction save for Your mercy and grace,
Keep us faithful Lord, 'til we see You face to face!

"Take heart, I have overcome the world" Jesus said,
You who are alive who were lost in sin and dead,
Who believed and received God's gift in the manger,
I am coming soon, guard your heart from sin's danger!

To those who overcome and live for Me today,
They will eat from heaven's tree of life always,
For those who walk in truth in all they say and do,
A white stone with a new name will be given you.

To those who are steadfast in My will to the end,
Authority to rule with Me, my promise penned,
The right to the tree of life in heaven above,
Be faithful and endure, abiding in My love.

To those who overcome, not denying My Name,
You'll be a pillar in My house, there to remain,
Be not lukewarm or out of My mouth I will spew,
Fight the good fight and win the reward gained by few.

Open

Open your ears to hear the message of love,
Given to you from the Creator above,
A message of hope ever needed today,
Jesus Christ, the Saviour, born to make the way.

Open your heart to someone who'll always be there,
Believing in you, when no one else seems to care,
He does not love to get but loves with open hands,
Though you turn away, your sin He understands.

Open your eyes to see that Christ died for you,
You can't save yourself, there's nothing you can do,
Christ offers forgiveness and new life today,
It's yours to receive, and from sin turn away.

Open your hands to let go and let Him lead,
For He knows what lies ahead and what you'll need,
Keep your eyes on Him, for He gives the best view,
Of treasures beyond this earth awaiting you.

Good News

You are not alone; God is everywhere,
God hears, even the most feeble prayer,
God doesn't have favourites; He loves YOU,
He is faithful when no one else is true,
God is with you, even for the long haul,
Even if you blow it again and fall.

God gives you hope no one can take away,
In Christ the child, in a manger He did lay,
Freedom given from all our sin and shame,
As we cry out our need in Jesus' name,
He enters when asked, and gives us anew,
Life from above, something we cannot do.

God is all-knowing; He knows what is best,
I forget that and lose His peace and rest,
But God is merciful and reaches out,
Extending His love even when I doubt,
God is all-powerful; I need not fear,
He can conquer my mountains and draw me near.

God is the creator, I know where I'm from,
I don't have to lose my direction like some,
God's Word is truth in a world gone wrong,
Lighting my path as I travel along,
Sometimes things happen I don't understand,
But I know God's in control, holding my hand.

Life can be routine, or it can be ever changing,
As I've experienced God, He's done re-arranging,
God sees the big picture, and allowing His touch,
I've never been the same or been loved so much,
There have been valleys, but He saw me through,
Lifting me to mountains to catch His best view.

Someday I'll finish life's journey at last,
All struggles, sorrow and pain will be past,
Taking naught with me, all is left behind,
Only the love of Jesus, and with Him I find,
Life that will last for all eternity,
A hope and a future, waiting for me.

The Word

The living Word came down to dwell among men so very long ago,
In flesh, human form, the divine seed placed in a virgin's womb to grow,
Long past foretold to Adam, prophets, wise men and shepherds in a field,
God's Word fulfilled, The Saviour of the world has come, God Himself revealed.

The Word came to reach out with God's love to save those lost in sin and shame,
He walked upon this earth, worked with His hands, wept, grew tired; Jesus is His name,
He came as the True Light to a world in darkness, to show us the way,
In Him alone is life; for through Him all things were made and have their stay.

The Word - Jesus Christ - God, experienced suffering, rejection and pain,
He came to those He created, who refused Him again and again,
Unjustly treated, abandoned by all, He obeyed the Father's will,
Knowing that for our freedom from sin and death, His blood would have to spill.

The Word, Jesus Christ, laid down His life to pay the debt that our sin did owe,
He arose, conquering over sin, death, the grave and Satan our foe,
Giving the right to those who would believe and receive Him in their heart,
To become His children, born of God, a Spiritual birth, a new start.

The Word, God, The Alpha, The Omega, The Beginning and The End,
King of Kings, Lord of Lords, Righteous One, Prince of Peace, Counsellor and Friend,
There is none other, under Heaven or Earth, all else shall pass away,
Christ promised to come back and take His own, won't you come to Him today?

The Wonders of His Grace

O the wonders of God's grace.
That came to earth's fallen race,
Love displayed in such a way,
God's Son in a manger lay.

O the need we have within,
To rescue us from our sin,
There is nothing we can do,
To bring about freedom true.

O how well He knows our frame,
Every hair and our name,
There is naught He cannot see,
Or can't do for you or me.

For God holds all in His hand,
Our life, breath, the earth we stand,
He opens wide, arms of love,
Through His own Son from above.

O that we would see the star,
And follow Him where we are,
Lift up your eyes, He is near,
He calls to all who would hear.

There is none that stand aright,
Before Holy God in His sight,
We all fall short; we sin each one,
That's why God sent His only Son.

He alone could pay the price,
Christ the sinless sacrifice,
Laid down His life and rose again,
Conquered sin and death's domain.

From a Babe, a Saviour, King,
Life is what He's offering,
Forgiving all your sin and shame,
A new beginning and His name.

So, when you wrap the gifts galore,
The Greatest Gift is at your door,
God's Son, Jesus, is life's reason,
Won't you let Him in this season?

The Year 2000

2000 years ago, God sent hope down to Earth,
Delivered in a stable, was His own Son's birth,
A light to the darkness to dispel fear and gloom,
He is your salvation, have you any room?

2000 - the year coming, have we come so far?
Are we wise men, following the Bethlehem star?
Or are we lost, drawn to stars of our own choosing,
Going nowhere fast, and our lives we're losing.

There are many stars that call for our attention,
But only One offers Divine intervention,
The star of Bethlehem, Jesus Christ is His name,
Lives given to Him change and are never the same.

Times have changed; our seasons so much out of control,
What or who can we hold onto; what is the goal?
The Master plan was set out by God long ago,
Written down in "The Bible" so mankind could know.

Jesus is **The** Way, **The** Truth and **The** Life for man,
2000 years ago, or now, it's still God's plan,
God's calendar of life is hastening to an end,
Be ready, receive Christ, don't wait my friend.

Emmanuel - God with Us

Anger, pain and hurting people - to this He came,
Lives wrapped in cycles of sin, going on the same,
Heavy hearts, broken dreams, shattered lives askew,
Questions unanswered, groping blindly, what to do?

O sweet babe, from heaven's portals ringing aloud,
Good news to mankind, there is hope o'er sins dark shroud,
Salvation comes to bring direction to lost souls,
Pointing to The Way, The Truth, The Life – He bestows.

This life seems to move faster with each passing year,
No time given to reflect or treasure what's dear,
Expectations, demands, we seek to meet them all,
Not hearing Emmanuel, God with us - His call.

"Peace on Earth and Goodwill to Men", how can this be?
In a world of constant strife and man's own cruelty,
God with us, He alone can change the heart of man,
To restore, to rebuild, to set us free - He can.

Jesus lived among us, accepting life's not fair,
Not turning from His purpose, He alone could bear,
He entrusted and believed the Father's will was best,
Death on a cross, He arose, our sins' debt addressed.

Emmanuel awaits, softly calling your name,
Knowing that when you come, you'll never be the same,
For when you turn from sin and believe on the Son,
You will be made new, and true life will have begun.

Why do I Bother with the Christmas Season?

Why do I celebrate another Christmas season?
When this past year hasn't given me a great reason,
I have to tell you that on my own, it wouldn't be,
For I am weak, prone to wander and self-pity,
So, what causes my heart to praise and carry on?
When things look bleak and there's no one to depend upon,
I'm at the end of my resources, with empty hands,
And life just gets rougher, with overwhelming demands,
When I want to bail out, but I make the choice to stay,
Is isn't because I have it in me - there's just no way,
I have the person of Jesus Christ, who lives within,
In Him there is hope beyond this world of strife and sin.

Jesus was sent from heaven to a lowly manger,
From having it all, to nothing, He was no stranger,
He understood surrendering to the Father's will,
Trusting and believing that this was His job to fill,
He knows life can be unfair, and people can be cruel,
He still reached out in love, and people called Him a fool,
He walked the dusty roads for miles and met many needs,
People followed Him for good, and others for His deeds,
He knows the heart of man and how wicked it can be,
Filled with selfishness and pride, and what's in it for me,
He knows about rejection, from those He came to love,
But chose to be faithful to His mission from above.

He knows about pain and sorrow, He went to the Cross,
Laying down His life for man, seeing it gain not loss,
Desiring to bring lost souls, to the haven of rest,
Offering forgiveness of sin and of heaven's best,
To those that would receive Him, His arms are open wide,
With comfort and healing, listening ears to confide,

Love that never ends, and one who is faithful and true,
Power to rise above anything and make it through,
He takes broken lives and puts the pieces together,
For He has a plan, not just for now, but forever,
To make us His masterpiece, the best that we can be,
Filling with joy, peace and love, never to be empty.

Now, you know why I celebrate another season,
Even if September 11th happened again, I would reason,
I have life, peace and joy, that no one can take away,
Held in God's safe keeping, I am secure come what may,
I still have my struggles and the valleys up ahead,
Disappointments, trials, pain, and mountains that I dread,
But I am not alone; Jesus walks this life with me,
Guiding, directing, giving light on this road to see,
I am on a journey, and one day, I will be home,
No more tears or sorrow, or on this earth will I roam,
I am captive to no one, though some would even try,
For my spirit is set free, my soul has wings to fly,
My hope is in Jesus, not the world and all its fare,
The greatest Gift, salvation, which nothing can compare.

The Creator Came

Creator of the world - you came to a manger,
Unbelievable, awesome - what could be stranger?
Fullness of God - manifest in bodily form,
Taking a servant's role - going against the norm.

Submitting to a world that quickly turned its face,
Against Your outstretched arms and the offer of grace,
Eyes that looked beyond all the filth and sin of man,
To see value and worth because of love - He can.

Bringing light to a world that is so far off track,
That He came to point the way of how to get back,
Left on our own, we get lost again and again,
But in Him we are found and securely remain.

Our souls, when we listen, ache for a higher plane,
That only He can offer, for its heaven that we gain,
He knows all about us, how stubborn and so proud,
That He comes to us in love, with God's grace endowed.

This world offers happiness that runs out real fast,
But Christ offers inward joy that will always last,
For it's not of this world, but a gift from above,
Receiving Christ in your heart, you're filled with His love.

Men strive to achieve peace, yet wars still do persist,
For they seek it their own way, and God they resist,
Peace comes through Christ, His Son; there is no other way,
Confession brings forgiveness and peace that will stay.

Freedom in this day demands we all have our rights,
Which gives full reign to some horrific sights,
Of babies aborted and thrown out as garbage,
Or terrorists that kill in a senseless rampage.

True Freedom comes as we surrender our own will,
To the God who alone our future can fulfill,
He's the Alpha and Omega; He sees it all,
Everything's in His control, He has the last call.

Alone? No - God is with us reaching out today,
He is calling you - yes YOU - don't ignore Him I pray,
Christmas began with Christ, the gift who came for you,
Who ALONE can give you hope, love and life anew.

He Came Even Though He Knew the Whole Story

Jesus knew the whole story before He came down to this earth,
Leaving His throne to take on human form through a virgin birth,
His coming to an unwed teen brought gossip, reproach and shame,
This teen accepted God's will with praise, glorifying God's name.

Jesus purposed that He would be born in the lowliest estate,
Making sure the Inn was full when Joseph and Mary came late,
His first visitors weren't family but some shepherds nearby,
Who weren't expecting to be told good news from angels on high.

They had no gifts, yet gave Him worship, praise and a humble heart,
In a smelly stable, with animals, but thrilled to take part,
Later came the wise men bringing expensive gifts from afar,
They found the baby Jesus by following a special star.

King Herod was told a king had been born and gave way to fear,
Having all male children two and under killed by sword and spear,
Jesus knew that evil would rise up to strike out against the plan,
Of God giving His only Son to bring salvation to man.

Jesus grew up with siblings, family chores and learned a trade,
His desire was to please God His Father, and to that He prayed,
He didn't run off and do His own thing, but waited for God's will,
Waiting 30 years before He began His work to fulfill.

Jesus didn't have it easy on the road that was ahead,
Wandering over the countryside, no shelter or a bed,
He wasn't always understood and knew rejection firsthand,
But He kept pressing on with God's message throughout the land.

He knew about friendships that were dear and how they failed
To be there when He needed them when at the cross He was nailed,

Even when one He trusted, betrayed Him for money to gain,
Jesus still loved and carried on His calling, even in pain.

He knew He'd pay a debt He did not owe, for all of mankind,
Unjustly accused, beaten, forsaken, still with peace of mind,
For He knew who held His future, trusting God was in control,
He experienced death for us and claimed freedom Satan stole.

He triumphed over the darkness and the struggle against sin,
He heard the deepest cry of man and now reaches deep within
To draw each soul to freedom's shore and give joy that is His own,
IMMANUEL, God with us, no more battles to face alone.

So, Jesus knew the whole story before He ever came here,
Even planned it thousands of years ago, waiting year after year,
I don't know my whole story, but God holds it in His hand,
I just pray for faithfulness to follow all that He has planned.

So, I guess when I'm feeling that my life is always on hold,
I'll read God's Word of men and women and their trust I am told
Was anchored in His faithfulness and believing He was there,
How they trusted their God for the unknowns of why, when and where.

I read of Abraham, who was called to leave all that he knew,
Relatives, friends, his home town, to a place where he had no clue,
Then trusted God without wavering that he would have a son,
With Sarah and him in their nineties, what God promised was done.

So, I have felt like Abraham leaving all and not knowing,
Of what's ahead and where I will eventually be going,
Our God is the same, and He promised to provide a place,
A God of miracles and wonders, I marvel at His grace.

I'm glad I don't know the whole story, I would have given up,
I would have said like Christ, "Father, can't you take away this cup?"
Yet for all that I have gone through, God has given peace and rest,
I wouldn't trade this walk with God, for He only seeks my best.

Why?

Creator of the universe, I marvel at your plan,
To come to earth in human form to reach the heart of man,
You came in such a quiet way, aside from all the crowd,
God Almighty, lowly, humble, not demanding or proud.

Why do I follow and obey this Saviour of mankind?
What has He to offer that I would leave all else behind?
My heart has been captured with a life born to die,
A love that reaches my inmost being and answers the why.

I remember as a child, the questions within my soul,
Why was I created, something's missing – I don't feel whole,
I searched and questioned, believing "there had to be more"
Than growing up, college, a job, marriage, kids and death's door.

I tried different churches – yet they did not hold the truth,
Until I was invited, to a gym night by some youth,
They had something that I needed, a wholeness deep inside,
They had found the answer to life; my soul had been denied.

What was the answer that I found so many years ago
That has always kept and drawn my heart back and made me so?
Giving me no peace, no rest when I strayed to other ways,
For there is only one path that leads to truth and always.

The lover of my soul, my creator, Saviour and friend,
The answer is in Jesus – whom God the Father did send,
Through a Babe, the Christ of Christmas was born to bring me life,
Divinity for humanity to save from death and strife.

I made a choice back then to ask Jesus Christ in my heart,
One I've never regretted, for He gave me a new start,
He made me whole, forgave my sin, I now have forever,
It's not about me, gaining the world or being clever.

God's word states we were created for Him and His glory,
He provides a way to know Him - through salvation's story,
Not through anything we can do, nor do we deserve His love,
But, because of grace and mercy, He beckons from above.

Another year past, traveling closer to heaven's shore,
Growing deeper in love with Jesus - who's given me more
Than anything or anyone this earth could seek to give,
In Him I have, I am, and for Him I'm called to live.

Take Away Christmas - Just Give Me Jesus

When the darkness is so dark and I cannot see my way,
Your star of hope breaks through, beckoning your light for my day,
There are times when I am overwhelmed; I cannot be moved,
You come and unclench my heart to trust – your love that's been proved.

You are never daunted by my fears, knowing each by name,
Your perfect love casts them out – they are gone from whence they came,
I cannot grasp tomorrow and today seems not enough,
You remind that it's not about me, or people, or STUFF!

Moments of wonder, joy and praise come right out of the blue,
And Your Spirit from within me is bursting out with YOU,
You are there, sometimes silent, and other times loud and clear,
Emmanuel – God with us, ever present, ever near.

There are days when I cry, "Why do you hide your face from me?"
Days when I feel that you have cast me off, You do not see,
There is no answer, no open doors and the walls close in,
I am to walk by faith, not by sight, for You are within.

You are my refuge and my shield, my hope is in Your Word,
The unfolding of your Word gives light; I won't be deterred,
To live for Jesus in a world that has cast Him aside,
Take away Christmas, just give me The Lord Jesus inside.

Take away the wrappings, glitter and the entire array,
I can't find Jesus – who actually created the day,
He was born in a manger, a barn to be exact,
Smelly animals, manure - nothing stately to attract.

Very basic, very real, and yet amazing, so profound,
Announced to shepherds hosting a choir of angelic sound,
God reached out His love to man, by sending His Son to earth,
There is hope beyond this world; through Jesus there is rebirth!

All of creation longs for new birth; it groans with its desire,
Earthquakes, floods, wars that ravage the land, heat, cold, snow and fire,
Aids, cancer, emptiness that demands more - yet never filled,
A treadmill of death, but through Jesus Christ, death has been stilled.

Take away Christmas; just give me Jesus; He came to die,
To take my sin and yours, to answer our hearts' deepest cry,
He paid the price on the cross for all our sin and shame,
Offering life forever, a new birth and a new name.

Christ' mas began with Christ, the baby Jesus, do you know?
Without Jesus, it's just STUFF, stress and warm feelings that go,
All the glitter wrapped up, needing to be filled up again,
Take away Christmas, just give me Jesus – He will remain.

The Heart of Christmas

Our hearts were created for passion and purpose beyond ourselves and this world,
And when left to our own devices, we fall short, fail and all hell comes unfurled,
The results are broken, wounded, hurting, empty, hard, proud, lost and hopeless hearts,
Existing, surviving, carrying on, even though fractured in so many parts.

Rejection, abandonment, loneliness drains away the passion or desire,
Finding yourself adrift, farther from the shore with the waves becoming higher,
Life becomes a struggle and you wonder what's the point, who really cares anyway,
Yet, on the horizon, a distant shore beckons; I am the answer, this way.

Paddling like mad in this new direction, you arrive to find it's a mirage,
All the rage, disappointment, frustration and feelings come on as an entourage,
You back paddle and set in motion another direction to fill the void,
Finding that again the ache is still there, regardless of what you had enjoyed.

The sun comes up and you think, ah better days lie ahead, surely, I'll be fine,
You bask in its rays, your heart warms up and life mellows to a taste of divine,
But then deep in your heart an increasing echo of emptiness drains your joy,
That which seemed your heart's desire has only been a fleeting moment to enjoy.

Your heart cries out, what is there left to fill this longing and emptiness within,
Who can heal your broken heart, who can put the pieces back, oh where to begin?
Then, you hear, the steady beating of a heart that is strong, full of life today,
The heart of Christmas, Jesus Christ, who offers to come into your heart to stay.

The baby lying in that manger was God come in the flesh so long ago,
God became a man, and with His heart, He reached out in love so that you would know,
This isn't all there is, and that He came to give your life purpose and passion,
He laid down His life for you, the God of mercy, forgiveness and compassion.

You see, our hearts were created for God, but our sin, by going our own way,
Separates us from God, bringing death that comes from inside and out decay,
For God so loves YOU that He gave His only Son, that if you believe in Him
You will not perish, but have everlasting life, with the true God, Elohim.

The Heart of Christmas, Jesus Christ, is knocking on the door of your heart today,
He desires to come in to heal and fill your heart, won't you let Him have His way?
Confess your sins to Him and acknowledge that He died to pay for all your wrong,
Open the door of your heart and ask Him in; He's been waiting there all along.

WHAT SHALL I GIVE YOU?

Shall I give you platitudes and silly words of rhyme?
Or lather you with frothy dreams of a better time?
I do declare if this is what I sought to bring to you,
You'd question my integrity, unwavering, untrue.
So, I shall tell you words of truth, God has brought to me,
Then you will know there is hope, beyond what you can see.

This year has been a journey, which stretched beyond belief,
I didn't think I'd make it, and begged God for relief,
He didn't bring me answers that brought an end in sight,
But walked me through the valleys, to see the mountain light,
To gain the faith perspective, that has an unseen view,
Trusting His past faithfulness continues to be true.

For God is not like me, failing flesh and weak at best,
He is strong and mighty, calling me to come and rest,
I can find in Him my peace, and strength to meet the day,
Knowing I can trust Him when there seems to be no way,
God holds all the answers and when my life seems a mess,
He is there to listen and bring comfort in my distress.

Life has been a struggle, but I have learned to grow,
It makes all the difference, of who you really know,
With all life's disappointments, I always have a choice,
To grow bitter and angry, or listen to God's voice,
There is nothing that happens that takes Him by surprise,
For He's always in control, and all knowing and wise.

I have known what it's like, to have and to have not,
Learning to release things, being content with my lot,
For what fulfills and completes, is not here on this earth,
But deep crying out to deep, met in man's rebirth,
That's why God gave us Christmas, despite what we believe,
God calls out His love to us, through Jesus to receive.

Without faith it's impossible to know this God of love,
You must believe He exists, and turn to Him above,
To place your faith here below will only come to be
An endless search of broken dreams, and futility,
There are many gods calling, and they are but a mist,
That swirl about to deceive but flee when you resist.

This world has many pathways that I could choose to take,
But I am called to live God's way, for there's much at stake,
For, beyond what I can see, this world is not the end,
God's call to eternity, I will have to contend,
There is heaven and hell, and the choice to be made,
Bears out who I live for, and the foundation I've laid.

I found the babe of Christmas so many years ago,
Who then became my Saviour, whose precious blood did flow,
To pay the price of my sin so I could come to God,
Exposing all the other "ways" to be but a fraud,
For He alone can forgive and bring me life anew,
Giving joy and a peace, which will always carry through.

I have seen His hand of mercy, time and time again,
Even with my doubts and fears, He's promised to remain,
Keeping me along this road, that always seems uphill,
I wouldn't keep on going, if it wasn't for His will,
I've experienced His blessings, just around the bend,
And His unfailing goodness, He never fails to send.

Can I do it on my own? At times I was so sure,
But doors just kept closing and I felt so insecure,
For I have been created to need His hand below,
To bring me closer to Him, so I would really know,
He loves me and He's there, and can fill every part,
With wholeness and completeness, with Jesus in my heart.

So, these gifts of truth I have, I give it all to you,
To ponder, to question, and discover what is true,
I know God is waiting, and listens to the prayer,
Of one who is seeking, and desires His loving care,
Why not come today, for you've nothing to lose,
Only everything to gain, if it's Jesus you choose.

Strange - But True

Another Christmas, what more can I say,
That hasn't been said, in so many a way,
My mind is a blank and I've struggled to write,
Of what God would say of that blessed night.
How does it relate to this day and age,
With the culture of self being the rage?

For God to come down in a lowly estate,
Defies all our reason and brings much debate,
For the God that we need to bring us relief,
Would not be a baby to carry our grief,
For what can He offer, this helpless pure child?
In a world that is dark, with hearts so defiled.

It says in God's word, our wisdom is naught,
With all our knowledge, that we have been taught,
Has never been known, to save our lost soul,
Or mended the broken, and made them whole,
The wisdom we have, is fleeting at best,
Which changes with seasons and gives no rest.

So, our eyes cannot see, nor dare understand,
A star in the East and the purpose God planned,
It all seems so foolish, to really believe,
That God would desire, our hearts to receive,
Dear God, I confess, this couldn't be stranger,
That hope could come from a Babe in a manger!

To live and to die, rejected by men,
Today the same story, as it was then,
There is no room at the inn of our heart,
We're filled with ourselves, in every part,
For all our good deeds that we would proclaim,
Are nothing to God, without Jesus' name.

Jesus rose from the dead, and lives today,
To offer forgiveness and a new way,
Our sin keeps us bound until we confess,
We're sinners in need of His righteousness,
Jesus blood on the cross covers our sin,
Why not answer His call and let Him in?

I do not deserve God's ongoing grace,
He freely bestows each day in my place,
That He would so care to know my name,
And wrap His strong arms around my weak frame,
Oh, I cannot grasp a love that's so deep,
That reaches down here, my soul to keep.

I am so amazed that He hears my voice,
Caring so much that I'd know His choice,
Life can be hard, and I stumble so much,
But He is there to uphold with His touch,
I do not know, for I just cannot see,
All that my Father has planned for me.

I only know that each step I would take,
Is much closer to eternity's wake,
For God holds me fast, as I'm prone to stray,
With my fears that would cloud the narrow way,
My heart and my mind are so oft at war,
Waiting and trusting for what You've in store.

For my weary eyes have such dim vision,
Of spirit works, of Your planned decision,
To all that You, God, have designed to do,
To shine Your glory in my life for You,
Again, I ponder, what could be stranger,
That hope comes from a babe in a manger.

So, Babe of Christmas, I've known through the years
The Saviour and God that conquers all fears!
God who is wisdom, above all mankind,
Creator of all, and light to the blind,
For all that we have, we're poor as can be,
Without Jesus, God, life will be empty.

I will tell you it's hard this new life divine,
Surrendering all, to walk a straight line,
You'll find your journey is against the grain,
T'will be marked with trials, along with pain,
The road is narrow to heaven's doorway,
But there is such joy, receive Him today.

The Journey

Where am I travelling, I've wondered over the years?
With all of the valleys, mountains, joys, sorrows and tears,
I had such dreams and plans I believed were really good,
But life hasn't always turned out, as "I think it should",
So, let me share as a pilgrim like you on life's road,
What treasures of wisdom, the Lord on me has bestowed.

My life is a journey of time, between birth and death,
I can choose to live it fully, with every breath,
Knowing each day is a moment of my history,
Of choices made, good or bad, towards my destiny,
Destiny, something fulfilled with steps taken each day,
Thankful I can choose to ask God to direct my way.

My childish heart still cries out "God, are we almost there?"
How many more dead ends, with no answer to prayer?
All the world that surrounds me mocks this place I am in,
"I love you Lord, as I am, such as I am," wearing thin,
You call me to trust, and remind me, home is not here,
What the world deems success, one day, will all disappear.

Time, waiting, and seasons, what has it all been about?
Becoming, not arriving, which shows without a doubt
I don't have the whole picture, but God sees the full view,
Of the life He has in mind for me, the best and true,
For God redeems the losses and makes a new picture,
One that is full and rich with a splash of adventure.

How does He do it, making life beyond the trenches?
Bringing beauty and a sweet fragrance in the stenches?
Moving me out, beyond what I can see before my face,
Giving me joy, peace, hope and contentment in this place?
Well, that's a story that lives on, through all of the years,
Of God coming to earth to make an end to our fears.

For in the town of Bethlehem, a star shone above,
A light in the darkness, pointing the way to God's love,
Born in a stable, was not the plan Mary would choose,
But God didn't hide it, having angels shout the good news,
Immanuel, God with us, the gift of His own Son,
Who would offer salvation from sin to everyone.

So, the God of creation, Jesus, lived on this earth,
Experienced troubles and struggles right from His birth,
Never did His own thing, making God's will His ambition,
Waiting 30 years before completing His mission,
During which He went through all the stages and trends,
Growing, living life, with family, neighbours and friends.

He grew in wisdom and stature, and favour with man,
He was perfect, not proud, with no thought of better than,
Bent on revealing the Father, so the world would know,
There is hope for today, and for each tomorrow,
Hope outside of people, ourselves and circumstances,
Secure in God's hand to our heart, not fate or chances.

If all that life offered was to be born and then die,
Then, what is the point, would be my lament and cry,
For deep within, in the darkest part of our soul,
We are broken, and only Jesus can make us whole,
For the world cannot repair what our sin has destroyed,
So, God sent His Son, making sin's power, null and void.

When Jesus turned thirty, He then began to proclaim,
"I am the way, truth and life" the God man who became
The Saviour, Redeemer, who took the sin of the world,
Who was nailed to a cross, where darkness gloated and swirled,
Died and rose again – three days later, out of the grave,
This Jesus overcame death and has the power to save!

Lift up your head, the Christmas child is alive today!
Who offers you life, a journey of a better way,
A road less travelled, but has a better view ahead,
Forgiveness paving the road, with heaven's golden thread,
Faith in Jesus, accepting what God has done for you,
Will open your eyes to hope, joy and love, all year through.

Christmas calls out, to the lost child in every heart,
Open the door and let God's gift of Jesus impart,
No longer lost, but found where you'll always belong,
Wrapped in His arms, that on your behalf, are always strong,
Never alone again, on this journey He is there,
Guiding His own, until they meet on Heaven's stair.

GRACE

When I look back over the days of my life past,
How slow at the time, and now marvel how fast,
All of the memories of where I have been,
I could not have imagined nor could have foreseen,
The fullness, the depth of all God brought me through,
Realizing how limited my point of view.

The world would tell me my value isn't much,
Because I haven't accomplished such and such,
But the longer I live and look all around,
People seem to strive ahead but gain no ground,
For when they arrive where they think they should be,
It's never enough and their souls are empty.

I have seen life with many setbacks and delays,
Fighting to find my way in life's twisted maze,
Making wrong turns because I just couldn't wait,
Weary, broken and back at the starting gate,
I cried out to God, "which way, what is your will?"
He answered again, "you must wait and be still".

In a world that is pressing with increased speed,
It's hard to hear and know the most urgent need,
So much to do, so little time, we can't hear,
God calling to unfulfilled longings and fear,
We frantically search and run with the crowd,
And life's demands become increasingly loud.

To wait, be still, goes against all my reason,
But, with God, there is a time and a season,
Not governed by man, nor a clock of demand,
His purpose for life goes beyond what I've planned,
From beginning to end, He sees the whole view,
So, how can I not trust Him to see me through?

The enemy of this world, taunts why I believe,
"Your God is not answering, you are naïve,
To trust and expect when there is nothing in sight,
God has simply left you in your well-deserved plight,
You stumble and sin and cry out for His grace,
But He will not hear you, oh child of disgrace!"

"You're not going to make it, so why not give up?
Accept what it is and drink life's bitter cup".

But I had come so far, and I could not conceive,
My Saviour and God would abandon and leave,
His word reminds me that I am a sinner at best,
There is no goodness in me that will stand the test,
He alone is good, and through His righteousness
I have a steadfast hope and His forgiveness.

I have faltered more now than I thought I would,
Revealing how His grace has certainly withstood,
There is no way to explain why or comprehend,
How faithful He's been more than family or friend,
I do have God, who despite all my heart's failings,
Will shepherd me back from my many derailing's.

So, why do I tell you my struggles in plain view?
I want you to know that my God still remains true,
For all through the ages, the message is the same,
One of hope and life found only in Jesus' name,
None other can break the power of sin's dark hold,
None other can change lives and give freedom untold.

No other 'god' has come down to become a man,
Setting aside His rights to exchange a loved filled plan,
Demonstrating love in a world that gave Him hate,
He died on a cross to pay for our sinful state,
He rose again and is alive today walking this earth,
In the lives of His children, like me, through new birth.

Only He can change lives and make hearts right within,
Only He can offer forgiveness for our sin,
Only He can take away the guilt and the shame,
Only Jesus gives life and power through His name,
Only Jesus is the anchor that holds secure,
For now, and eternity, His love will endure.

Dear friends, my life is a testimony of His glory,
Of His sustaining grace ever weaving His love filled story.

Snowflakes

Sometimes like the snowflakes that dance and swirl outside my windowpane,
I can move with complete abandon to life's rhythm and refrain,
Allowing the unseen hand to carry me to heights where I soar,
Filling me with a melody that awakens my soul for more.
I can move with the notes, be it sweet or melodic in its tune,
Or rest in life's setbacks or hold with a longing will this end soon?

But there are times, like the snowflake, I am weighed down and I get stuck,
The layers begin to build and get shoveled with all my life's muck,
Sometimes, I'm good for a snowman that rolls together in a ball,
Creating a momentum of joy for others, I can stand tall,
But when the rays of heat beat fast and relentless upon my brow,
My form is changed, despite my efforts to hold fast and disallow.

So, when life becomes a puddle, from a solid I could define,
I long for where I was, or should be, and discontented I pine,
I fail to see the purpose that this new state could offer much,
There isn't much substance, or future, and to my anger I clutch,
But then in my despair, a small bird comes to my puddle to drink,
I was laid bare for its refreshment, causing my heart to rethink.

What if like the snowflakes that dance and swirl outside my window pane,
Having many patterns, sizes and functions that they all contain,
Were but a glimpse of Heaven's whisper of hope to my searching heart,
Of a Master Designer, who fashions me and knows from the start
The beauty my life can take on isn't limited to one way,
It's a symphony in the making, this life that I live today.

What is this beauty that God longs to give to each one on the earth?
Where is the hope for weary hearts and creation's cry for rebirth?
Each year I 'm reminded as the Christmas season beckons to all,
God sent His Son to extend hope and love; that is His encore call,
On our own, the curtain of sin drapes over, concealing His face,
But with the Christ Child, the light pierces through with mercy and grace.

Just like the snowflakes glittering at night above the moonlit sky,
God's message proclaims through the darkness, man no longer needs to die,
The light from the heavenlies came down as a babe in a manger,
God, this Jesus, took on a created shape, what could be stranger?
A divine purpose foretold that would redeem the lost sinful heart,
Offering new life, and freedom to move forward with a fresh start.

So, I move forward and with my hand in His, I continue on,
Sometimes I hear Heaven's song and wonder what's next to come upon,
Other times, there is only stillness and I long to hear His voice,
But I can choose to believe, and I can choose to praise and rejoice,
Trusting He will hold me together; in my weakness, He is strong,
Transforming me to His beauty, in all seasons, my whole lifelong.

Christmas Joy Again - Why?

I can't tell you that this year has been one that I would want to live again,
I can tell you that it has been one of ups and downs with mixed joy and pain,
At times I cried out to God, and said, Lord, it is enough, please make it stop,
But God just kept giving out His grace to this weak and miserable sop.

I can't say that I have arrived and look back with joy untold from what I learned,
I will admit that I can whine with the best, yet in my heart another page turned,
I am not where I was, I have changed for the better, and I am yet to where I could be,
My Father has great expectations, and a love that just simply does not give up on me.

I can't tell you that I am the greatest kid of His, nor am I one that sits without complaint,
I am so glad that My Father is slow to anger and has a great capacity for restraint!
For I am sure at times He is thinking, does she not know by now, after all these years
I have her best in mind, and long to wrap her in my arms and wipe away her tears?

Each time I try to settle, and want to plant my feet in firm, God moves the ground,
Reminding me again that it's only in Him that my anchor in life can truly be found,
I can't tell you that I've been thrilled; my plans once again are feathers in the wind,
And this subscription to my life, I would love at times, to cancel, change, or rescind!

However, or whatever, I keep learning AGAIN, today is all I am given,
It may be sunny, raining, relentless wind, or a raging storm that's snow driven,
A picture of this life with all its changing moments, but still my life in motion,
Never stagnant, I can't go backward, and what's with "It's a Wonderful Life" notion?"

Life, well, it isn't the 'things, people or me' that bring hope, for they will always change,
For they leave me stranded, alone AGAIN, picking up the pieces of my heart to rearrange,
But, as I stoop down and in the quiet moments where no one else can reach inside,
God meets me there, whispers I will always love you, and will never leave you cast aside.

At times, I have to admit, I put up walls and give Him silence for I am angry or numb,
But He is faithful to pursue, for His love is not based on me and I finally succumb,
Wondering why again, I run from the only one that has always been trustworthy and true,
I confess my sin and need of Him, and marvel at this grace He gives, no matter what I do.

He has stretched me beyond my limits, and my life has been at times hanging by a thread,
Whether finances, a place to live, a job, relationships, or my body rejecting my daily bread,
No matter how weak in mind, body or soul, God has been my strength whatever the need,
Providing, sustaining, uplifting, sometimes carrying, and enabling me to proceed.

Who is this God you ask, and what difference would He make should you call on His name?
He is the God of the universe, the one who created you, the Only God who personally came,
As a babe, in a manger, from Heaven to earth to reach out with a tangible hand of love,
Inviting you to know Him, experience the life you've never known, which comes from above.

This baby, Jesus, the Son of God, born in a family, lived in this world of such brokenness,
Experienced joy, sorrow, pain, loss, rejection, but never gave in to His flesh or hopelessness,
For He knew that He was sent with a mission to save a dying world that was eternally lost,
You and me, and to give us life, it would be death on a cross for our sin that it would cost.

For our sin, that sinful nature, separates us from the God who is holy, righteous and just,
God gave us Christmas, not Santa Claus or Happy Holidays, but a call to believe and trust,
This Jesus, the Saviour, who stands knocking, waiting to be invited into your life and heart,
Offers healing and forgiveness, and a right relationship with God no one can tear apart.

Life beyond the limits, joy beyond the pain, hope and peace in all
the turmoil we live,
Wrapped up in Christmas, the gift no matter what, is boundless and free in
all God has to give,
I know Him as my Saviour, and, *"It **IS** a wonderful life"* **because** Christ lives out in me,
The reason for life's seasons, meaning beyond myself...what keeps **you** from this journey?

God - Jesus - Do You Know Me?

Do you see the wonder that fills my heart when kindness chooses to knock at my door?
Do you hear the melody I sing in my soul for the birth of each child I bore?
Do you feel the passion and longings I have, that crave so much more than life can give?
Do you taste the sweetness of my dreams that are whipped with hopes that I desire to live?
Do you smell the fragrance of my life that I have left this world, down throughout the years?
Do you perceive the reason for my being and just what future course that it steers?
Do you touch who I truly am, a creation found in no other the same?
Do you know Me, a human so far from heaven, do you even know my name?

Do you see the growing darkness that continually seeks to invade my soul?
Do you hear the lies that taunt me daily, incessant as a pounding drummer's roll?
Do you feel the fears that build walls I cannot climb, trapping me deeply from within?
Do you taste my bitter tears of disappointment, served to fill each year that weigh in?
Do you smell the sweat of my life's struggles that bear down to bring me to my knees?
Do you perceive the battle my heart wages, good versus evil, sin's deadly disease?
Do you touch where deepest shame abides, but longs to be loved, forgiven, and set free?
Do you know what flesh and blood struggle with truly; I ask, can you, do you KNOW me?

Do I, the living God, creator of all, see, hear, feel, taste, smell, perceive, touch, know?
How can I understand, being God, not a human and living on earth below?
Lend me your ear and I will speak to your heart, mind and soul, opening your eyes,
For I who have created every part of you, you in my likeness, typifies,
I who fashioned your beating heart, do I not know the joy and pain that it holds?
I who gave you the breath of life, do I not know your own story as it unfolds?
Do your ears not hear the sounds of my creation that speak of My presence on earth?
Do you not experience my touch, and feel the gift of wonder at each new birth?

Have I not answered the deepest need, God with You, Jesus, my Son in human form?
Sharing in your humanity, in all ways made like you, but brought forth out of the norm,
His conception from heaven, the Most High overshadowed the virgin Mary's womb,
Came to your world, full of darkness, unbelief, and desperate hearts closed with no room,
Born in a barn full of animals, with only straw to cradle this baby's head,
But a choir of angels rejoicing, shepherds and wise men I sent calling instead,
Back then, even then, evil rocked His world and terror sought to extinguish the light,
But I AM God, and I reign over darkness, for your Salvation was born at night.

I have walked this earth, raised in a family where I laughed, cried, played and grew up,
I found out what it felt like to be different, not belong in this world's lineup,
I set aside my glory, and experienced the limitations that flesh gives,
I grew weary, hungry and was tempted to succumb to Satan's lies and motives,
I did it all right, I never sinned, yet, coming to my own, I was not received,
It hasn't changed, sin rails against, runs or hides from the light, for man's heart is deceived,
I know love, joy, anger, grief, rejection, abandonment and the ultimate loss,
From family, friends, neighbours and religious ones, and what it means to bear a cross.

The cross, yes, I came to demonstrate my love for you, by dying in your place,
I took all your sin, the shame, the guilt, the penalty of your sin to offer grace,
You see, my birth is Christmas, Me, the greatest gift wrapped in love for you,
Sent to break the power of sin, transforming and changing, something you can't do,
A gift that offers freedom, from all that would trap you and keep you from becoming,
All that I have created you for, Knowing Me, Life, Your own special calling,
I rose again, conquering sin and death, so even when evil rears its ugly head
With terror and lies, remember, I have overcome, I'm alive, I AM NOT DEAD!

I came for you to KNOW Me, for your name has been engraved on the palm of my hand,
Before the world began, I knew you, your life that you think you control or command,
I have walked through your life, you have never been alone, I have been there all along,
In the good times, the tough times, my pursuing faithful love has been
heaven's sweet song,
I have brought you to deep places, and in the quiet, we have grown so close together,
In knowing Me, your eyes will be opened beyond yourself to a life forever,
I stand each day, and I knock at the door of your life, waiting to be asked in,
Remember who I AM, open up, I KNOW you by name, is there room at your inn?

The Tree

It's that time of year again and I pull out the Christmas tree,
All folded up in a box, having no semblance of what it will be,
I lift out the base which will hold all the branches and décor,
Then sort all the branch sizes in several piles on the floor,
I begin to build the tree fanning out the branches as I go,
Watching it emerge far beyond the boxed beginnings below,
I have to say a real tree was so much easier than this,
And, how can I forget the tree scent that I really do miss!

Finally, it's complete and I stand back to look and assess,
It isn't perfect and has several places of more and less,
I then seek out some lights to bring some glow to its dull frame,
And after much rearranging, well, it just isn't the same!
I then pick up strands of beads, several sets of white and red,
Wondering why I bought so many to twist and to thread,
Weaving all around the branches, the tree begins to bloom,
Coming to life with such beauty, displayed in my living room.

I have yet to place my ornaments to garnish my Christmas tree,
Gifts I received each year, that hold such a special memory,
Each one is so placed, for where it would best fill and do its part,
Of displaying love that was given, from each and every heart,
I also find paper handprints from two Grandchildren of mine,
And another ornament with, a Grandbaby footprint design,
So many years of Christmas to ponder over in my mind,
Decorating trees with family, with family love intertwined.

I now turn to find, there are no more ornaments to unpack,
And there aren't any empty spots that my tree has a lack,
So, finally it's time to place, the tree topping of a star,
A symbol of light to all, of those that are near and afar,
To cause our eyes to look up, beyond the glitter and décor,
With a light in the darkness, to find a message there is more,
Of the gift of hope that is offered, to each and every one,
Emmanuel, God with us, in the Christ Child, God's only Son.

So, I stand back from the tree and I start to ponder the thought,
Of what the gift of Christmas is, that even the wise men sought,
Why put up a tree, how does it fit with the Christmas story?
This Babe in a manger, and angel choirs singing His glory,
I think of the wrapped gifts, expressing our love under the tree,
And of John 3:16, "That God so loved the world" ...yes, you and me,
That He gave the greatest gift, His love wrapped up in a baby,
I don't have a manger, shepherds, or wise men, but I have a tree...

This tree is a tradition that came to join our Christmas cheer,
Another way we can celebrate this special time of year,
A time we gather together where we place our gifts of love,
Loving and giving, which came by example from God above,
God is love, and His love is one that will never leave nor end,
A love that meets us in our brokenness with power to mend,
Bringing light to our darkness and opening our eyes to see,
Christmas isn't the tree or gifts, but God Himself to you and me.

Our story began with God forming us from the dust of the ground,
From a world He created, where plants and living creatures abound,
From nothing to something, He made all the heavens and the earth,
But only to man, He gave the gift of immeasurable worth,
Created in His likeness, with a heart, mind and soul with free choice,
Nothing else in creation was given, such a place or a voice,
Placed in the garden called Eden, where all was provided and good,
God also placed two trees, with a message man clearly understood.

"The Tree of life" and "The Tree of the knowledge of good and evil"
Were a choice of "Life" or doing it "My Way" with no return or retrieval,
God gave us freedom to decide whether we would trust and obey,
Giving us His best, He did not push, nor manipulate to sway,
A choice was made of "My Way", to believe that God withheld His best,
Choosing Satan, a liar and the deceiver, man lost his rest,
For sin entered his soul, and death, fear and shame began its reign,
God's heart was broken, but God had a love that sin could not restrain.

God did not abandon, but pursued mankind with love through the ages,
Offering life, written down in the Bible throughout all the pages,
A promise of a Saviour, who would break the power of sin and death,
God sent His only Son, the God-man that gave with His last breath,
To pay our debt, He died on a rugged cross made from a tree,

Three days later, He arose from the dead to prove the victory,
Death was defeated, sin's power broken with all its guilt and shame,
Forgiveness and life are offered to those who trust in Jesus' name.

So, I have a tree, but the call at Christmas is which tree you will believe,
The Tree of Life God offers is Jesus, will you trust and receive?
Trusting the One who made and loves you, has only the best in mind,
Who is faithful, all knowing, with a plan uniquely for you designed,
Or The Tree of the knowledge of good and evil, myself, "My Way",
How is that working for you, believing lies of Eden's replay?
Satan still deceives and lures hearts that are bent on their own choice,
To a lost eternity because of turning away from God's voice.

I have a tree, The Tree of Life, found in Jesus, the Christmas child,
He is The Way, The Truth and The Life, through Him I am reconciled
To God, I am forgiven and promised life that is forever,
I am loved, with a love that nothing or no one here can sever,
There are many voices, and life has many paths that I could choose,
But I look back at Eden, and today, there is too much to lose,
I choose Life, and to listen to the only true trustworthy voice,
There are two trees before you this Christmas – which tree will be your choice?

The Christmas Interruption

Interruptions, never convenient, unexpected, not in the schedule or
what I had planned,
Out of the blue, a small event or one that capitulates into an
all-consuming demand,
Most times annoying, irritating, but then comes along "the one" that stops
me dead in my tracks,
It can be a miracle, a joy, or "the one" that overtakes my body in
deep sobbing wracks,
Life can be so 'normal', 'routine' and you can't imagine otherwise than what it
has always been,
But then come the 'interruptions' reminding me I am not in control
of the unforeseen.

Ordinary, me, nothing special and yet there can be those defining moments
that I say yes,
And it's then God steps in and creates a picture of His beauty and grace
in my brokenness,
He carries me in the storms when the waves are bent on taking me to the
bottom of life's sea,
Granting me strength in my weakness, and protection of my heart and mind
of fears that threaten me,
Taking me places I would not willingly have gone, as I keep clinging to the
known so tightly,
And, I find I am moving forward partaking in a plan that goes beyond
my own story.

Why is it, looking back, I can see the greatest joy amidst deepest
pain and sorrow?
Did I sense it all then going through another interruption of my life?
A resounding NO!

Was it not like the Master painter slashing out strokes of colour on a stark
and barren canvas?
Revealing a picture that developed with time, persistence, for a meaning
it would encompass,
What is it all about, where is lasting meaning, hope and enduring joy to be
found on this earth?
It is found with God interrupting the world and a virgin's life with
'Christ' mas, The Saviour's birth.

Over 2000 years ago, an angel sent by God interrupted a young
Jewish girl's day,
It was an ordinary day, nothing that prepared her for a miracle
coming her way,
A life changing one, not just for her, but for all mankind and future
generations to come,
That she would be with child, The Son of God, was hard to fathom and in her
heart found troublesome,
How could this be she asked, being a virgin, as this was beyond her
human comprehension,
The angel spoke of the sovereignty and power of God, His creative
life-giving dimension.

His spirit would come upon her with the power of The Most High, bringing forth life from above,
And let her know nothing is impossible with God, O blessed and favoured one of His love,
Mary said yes, believing, trusting and surrendering her will to the God interruption,
Even though amidst the joy, against her would come ridicule, shame, unbelief with great disruption,
Her life would never be the same and neither did she know that this Son would bring her deepest grief,
For the cross yet ahead that He would bear, carrying her sin and all mankind for eternal relief.

The 'Christ' mas interruption, "For God so loved the world that He sent His only Son" to die,
To pay for the sin of mankind, that if they would believe and receive life was the Father's cry,
They would not perish in this world of darkness, emptiness, without hope or light to guide their days,
The Saviour, the gift of life itself, redeeming us from ourselves in our lost and erring ways,
This Christmas, let Christ interrupt your life with the greatest gift you will ever receive,
Would this be your defining moment saying yes 'in the Christ child" The Saviour, I will believe?

FOREVER

Christmas is about forever, of hope and life that will never end,
A gift that keeps on giving far more than you could ever comprehend,
Unwrapping all our hopes and dreams to meet longings deep within our heart,
Our creator God sends a child, His only Son, His love to impart,
To our souls that wander and seek to find that which is needed most,
Restoration, wholeness, a restored relationship with our Maker foremost.

Christmas is about forever, of lasting peace this world does not know,
Coming from The Prince of Peace, Jesus, who would pay the price to bestow,
For our sin, rebellion against God, severed peace for all of mankind,
Strife, envy and death came to us with all creation, our groans aligned,
The babe of Christmas, the only one that could become our peace with God,
The perfect holy one that could pay sins price came to dwell on earth's sod.

Christmas is about forever, of boundless joy not obtained through man,
The source is God, in Him, about Him, from Him, complete, never less than,
Joy inexpressible, filled with glory, offered through the Son of God,
Angels rejoicing, shepherds in awe, their worship in heart did applaud,
Sent by the Father, born of a virgin and laid in a manger low,
Sweet baby Jesus, gift of God's joy for hearts that are open to know.

Christmas is about forever, of hope overflowing with power,
Springing from the God of Hope, though man endeavours through his willpower,
With constant striving, never enough, no secure anchored hope on earth,
Hope in hope, hoping, seeking, never coming to a safe harboured berth,
God's hope for mankind, Jesus, calling out to all adrift on life's sea,
Come, come, you who are weary, find rest and hope found only in Me.

Christmas is about forever, The Light streaming from Heaven afar,
That pierces through the darkness shining with glorious light none can bar,
For He is the way, the truth and the life, who alone conquered sin and death,
On a cross He paid sin's price and said "it is finished" with His last breath,
The Lamb of God, perfect, took our punishment for sin and rose again,
Breaking the power of darkness, His light will never cease to remain.

Christmas is about forever, of love that's beyond all we could dream,
While yet sinners we're loved just as we are, no goodness in us would deem,
A love that breaks the power of sin and gives the sinful heart the key,
To life, forgiveness found in Jesus and no longer captive but free,
Now no separation from God and born anew deep within our soul,
A new creation, the old passed away, the broken becoming whole.

Christmas is about forever, Jesus, The Lord, lives forever more,
The High Priest of Heaven who for His own will never cease to implore,
His Spirit indwelling each with power to live anew sharing His love,
Awaiting the promised return of The King coming soon from above,
He will come quickly, the day is almost spent, can you see the signs?
Do not tarry, come while The Light of Christmas in this world still shines.

Printed in the United States
By Bookmasters